for **Donna Rose**

My valiant friend.
In your quiet turns and consistent efforts,
you have demonstrated that life is what
you choose to make it,
not what a prognosis says it is.

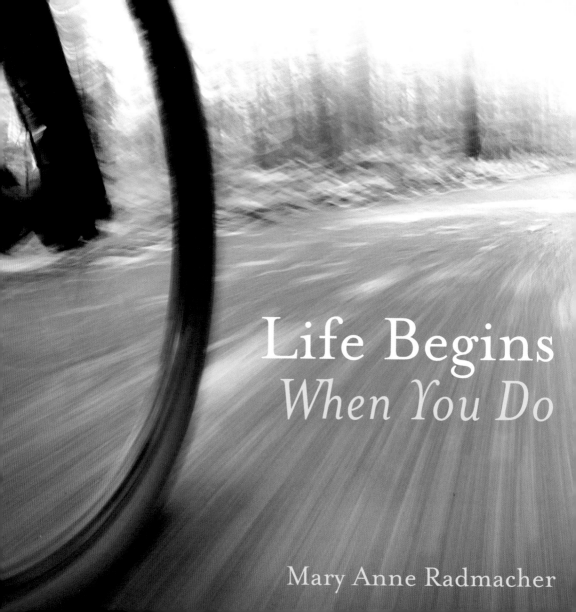

Life Begins
When You Do

Mary Anne Radmacher

Copyright © 2011 by Simple Truths (layout)
Published by Simple Truths
1952 McDowell Road, Suite 300
Naperville, Illinois 60563
800-900-3427

Simple Truths is a registered trademark.

Design: Jared McDaniel, Studio430.com
Images: Jeff Vanuga
ThinkStock.com
iStockPhoto.com
Author photo: © 2011 Michael Stadler

Printed and bound in the United States of America

ISBN 978-1-60810-121-4

03 WOZ 12

Table *of* Contents

Introduction

"Nothing ever becomes real until
it is experienced. Even a proverb
is no proverb until your life
has illustrated it."

JOHN KEATS

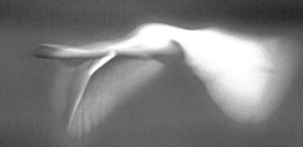

"The true perfection of man
lies not in what man has,
but in what man is."

OSCAR WILDE

FOR DECADES I HAVE MEASURED MY DECISIONS AND BEEN DEFINED BY MY POEM, MY STATEMENT OF PURPOSE—**LIVE WITH INTENTION**.

Live With Intention

Walk to the edge.

Listen hard. Laugh. Play with abandon.

Practice wellness.

Continue to learn.

Choose with no regret.

Appreciate your friends.

Lead or follow a leader.

Do what you love.

Live as if this is all there is.

P rior to writing my core values in this way, I lived by the wise sentiments and guidance captured in quotes written over the centuries. From the first gift of such quotes from my summer camp friend, Russell, called *Apples of Gold and Wings of Silver,* I have found the finest instruction in these condensed statements…these simple truths.

Since I was 14 years old, I have been collecting and learning from quotes. I heard about the practice of creating a "commonplace book" years after I began gathering the lyrics, poems and phrases that impacted me. Thomas Jefferson followed the time-honored practice of maintaining such a book, which gathered the significant lessons and life-impacting statements of traveling instructors, singers and poets. Essentially an individual's commonplace book records the curriculum of his or her life—the things that someone considers important enough to write down, revisit and continue to study.

In this book, you will see a portion of my collection of quotes. I encourage you to begin your own practice of a commonplace book. Maintaining one for your family is a wonderful way of communicating the significant lessons of your daily life.

I "met" the work of Mac Anderson as a young retail store manager. His small quote books had a strong appeal for me. I sold hundreds of those small books! The depth and focused purpose reflected in Mac's collections resonated with me and my habit of having aphorisms and quotes be some of my best teachers.

May these words light a fire for you to live close to your intentions. May they challenge you to act with certainty, as Mark Twain said,

"TWENTY YEARS FROM NOW YOU WILL BE MORE DISAPPOINTED BY THE THINGS THAT YOU DIDN'T DO THAN BY THE ONES YOU DID DO. SO THROW OFF THE BOWLINES. SAIL AWAY FROM THE SAFE HARBOR. CATCH THE TRADE WINDS IN YOUR SAILS. EXPLORE. DREAM. DISCOVER."

1

Live with intention.

Investigate and define your purpose, your "must."

Nearly everyone postpones one grand thing or a collection of mighty hopes and dreams.

Between the quote marks of our lives are phrases like these:

"When things slow down… when I finish my degree…when I get certified… as I acquire a deeper knowledge base… when I have kids… when the children are grown… when I get well… when I marry… when I divorce… when I retire… when I get that promotion, that raise, that job, that house, that whatever the fill-in-the-blank is for your specific postponing of life…"

YOUR LIFE BEGINS WHEN YOU DO.

You may think you are postponing the longing of your soul until life aligns itself with your vision, until elements conspire to be more favorable…but as it happens, life just lolls along at the same remarkable consistent and disinterested cadence. Life is impartial. YOUR personal, subjective life (dreams, satisfactions, contentment, achieve-ments, vision, fullness, passions, aspirations) begins when you begin.

From my teens into adulthood I said, "I want to be an artist." One day I changed the sentence to, "I am an artist." My view changed. Life began. I looked behind me and saw that I had been accidentally living as an artist. I had been laying down a path that was only now visible to eyes that had begun to see. Beginning my life as an artist made my heart's longing and the small, tentative labors of my hands— visible and tangible. I began by opening the door and simply believing that I could live my dream. I began living that dream simply by seeing that I could.

Your purpose, that thing that among the many to-dos of your days, is what you must do. Embrace the truth of your purpose each minute of your precious life…for how very true it is that life begins when you do.

If you would dream it
BEGIN it.

If you have an idea
OPEN it.

If there is longing
ACKNOWLEDGE it.

If there is mission
COMMIT it.

If there is daring
DO it.

If there is love
SPEAK it.

If there is resource
USE it.

If there is abundance
SHARE it.

Steve Maraboli, author and fellow life enthusiast, gave me permission to share this message with you:

I truly feel too many of us just go through life existing and not really living each moment. That type of existing has led countless people to look back at their lives with a sense of regret for a life not truly lived and enjoyed.

I have volunteered at many hospitals and spent the last moments with many people as they shared with me similar regrets. No one on their death bed has ever expressed to me that they wish they would have worried more, been more concerned about other's opinions, spent more time at work, or taken less chances. Instead, they had expressed a wish that there had been more chances taken, more kisses given, more hugs cherished, more love expressed, more laughs and a closer relationship with loved ones.

Too many people, in their latter days of life, have an aching sense of regret. Don't let that be so with you.

*What will you do with this moment, with today?
I'll tell you what I'm going to do:

I'm going to live every moment of today!
I'm going to seize every moment and truly embrace each blessing.
I will laugh and make others laugh.
I will share what I know and listen to what others know.
I will forgive myself and others for past mistakes.
I will be kind, generous and loving.
I will trust in God.
I will be a good friend.
I will do my best.
I will take chances.
I will express my love and appreciation for others.

Today I will live in such a manner that there will be no possible room for regret.
Then I'll do the same tomorrow.
Join me each day in this celebration of life.
We are all in this together.
Let's live with no regrets."

Steve Maraboli

TO CHANGE ONE'S LIFE:

1. Start immediately.
2. Do it flamboyantly.
3. No exceptions.

—WILLIAM JAMES—

"Only when we are no longer
afraid do we begin to live."

DOROTHY THOMPSON

"*It is more important to know where
you are going than to get there quickly. Do
not mistake activity for achievement.*"

MABEL NEWCOMER

*"Simply the thing I am
shall make me live."*

SHAKESPEARE

*"How wonderful it is that nobody need
wait a single moment before starting
to improve the world."*

ANNE FRANK

*"The unexamined life
is not worth living."*

SOCRATES

*"Many are stubborn in pursuit of the
path they have chosen,
few in pursuit of the goal."*

FRIEDRICH NIETZSCHE

CHAPTER TWO

Walk to the edge.

Begin as if you will finish.

"The journey of a thousand miles begins with a single step."

CHINESE PROVERB

True...but that pesky first step can be a killer, can't it? I love Will Rogers' quote, "Even if you're on the right track, you'll get run over if you just sit there." So many times we have great intentions. We're going to read a good book, write out our five-year life plan, start a new business, lose weight, learn a language. But for some reason, we can't quite get around to taking that first step.

We're all guilty of procrastinating. But here's the thing. Procrastinating when something is important, when it's something you know you should do, can drain your energy and you won't even know it.

> **"Procrastination is attitude's natural assassin. There's nothing so fatiguing as an uncompleted task."**

This quote by William James is instructive. There are times when I have difficulty setting aside blocks of time to write. I know I should be doing it. In fact, I even love doing it (once I get started), but...here we go...back to that pesky first step. When I need a "nudge," I visualize just how good I'm going to feel when I finish. I know I'll feel energized. Invigorated. I also know I'll feel proud that I did something about that which I was so resistant.

"SO MAKE A POINT TO FIND SOMETHING THAT WORKS FOR YOU WHEN YOU NEED A NUDGE TO GET STARTED."

MAC ANDERSON

HERE'S A GREAT EXAMPLE:

"What next?" the young, upwardly mobile mother of three asked when her lucrative contract job abruptly came to an end with a wholly unexpected industry layoff. Beyond the obvious, "What next?" question was a whole string of deeper questions, all of which began with "Why?" or "What?" and none had any ready answers. In the weeks that we worked together, Dyan realized that the apparent success of her career had kept her from walking to the edge of her own dreams and passions. She had deferred her dream to "some day" because the perks of the present job seemed to outweigh beginning on her own dreams. She created a statement of purpose and has graciously agreed to let me share it with you. The structure acknowledges the sense of season and change in her life and her desire to begin making her dreams come true now.

Dyan does indeed now begin as if she intends to finish...and she's allowed me to share the results of her exploration with you.

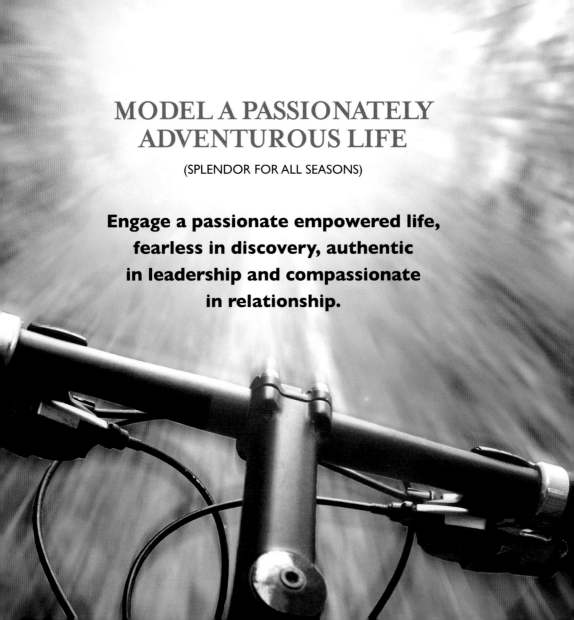

MODEL A PASSIONATELY ADVENTUROUS LIFE

(SPLENDOR FOR ALL SEASONS)

Engage a passionate empowered life,
fearless in discovery, authentic
in leadership and compassionate
in relationship.

SPRING:

LOVE prevails. FORGIVE unconditionally and be forgiven. Let FAITH cure doubt.

SUMMER:

LEARN to overcome ignorance with truth. LEAD, driven by vision, not ideology. INSPIRE yourself and others to leave a legacy.

AUTUMN:

Be relentlessly CURIOUS to solutions. Be FEARLESS while learning from failures. Be unfailingly AUTHENTIC and associate with people who are true.

WINTER:

CLARIFY with the soul. LISTEN, knowing that being understood is parallel to love. EMPOWER the intuitive heart and create.

"The only joy in the world is to begin."

CESARE PAVESE

"THE MOST EFFECTIVE WAY
TO DO IT, IS TO DO IT."

AMELIA EARHART

"Living at risk is jumping off the
cliff and building your wings
on the way down."

RAY BRADBURY

"IF LIFE WERE ETERNAL ALL INTEREST
AND ANTICIPATION WOULD
VANISH. IT IS UNCERTAINTY WHICH
LENDS IT SATISFACTION."

KENKO HOSHI

"DON'T ASSUME A DOOR IS
CLOSED; PUSH ON IT.
DO NOT ASSUME IF IT WAS
CLOSED YESTERDAY THAT
IT IS CLOSED TODAY."

MARIAN WRIGHT EDELMAN

CHAPTER THREE

Listen hard.

Learn to hear the silence
in between the notes.

There are so many ways to listen…and there's a relentless stream of things to listen to. A significant element of listening hard is knowing what is worth listening to. There is a lot of chatter. Noise. It begins with the chatter and noise in our own thinking and radiates outward. Music. Newscasts. Pre-recorded announcements. Even elevator rides come with a soundtrack.

I learned my best lesson in listening as a young secretary. New to the business world, I was eager to be excellent at every task. My employer showed me how to use a dictation machine to transcribe his letters, and he expected me to transcribe to a final copy. This was a different era of technology, so let me explain. He expected me to listen to his taped voice and type with precision to a final document with up to three carbon copies, without a first draft. Two errors were acceptable, but he preferred no errors. I didn't know how exceptional this request was. Since I didn't know any other secretaries, I didn't know this was outside professional norms. I transcribed accurately by closing my eyes and listening to every word—letting those words go into my ears and out my fingers with ease of motion. I listened intently to every inflection, every pause. Over time, I could literally see the keyboard and watch the words form as I listened to them. A year later, I was in the company of several high-level secretaries and administrative assistants. There I learned they always took dictation off the machine in draft form and then created their correct carbon copies from a corrected hard copy.

"How can you possibly do that?" they asked me, when they heard that I typed a final copy.

"I listen hard," I answered.

After I learned that what I did was considered next to impossible, I stopped being able to do it! But the lesson in listening hard in other areas of my life had already become a part of my practice.

That experience taught me that, "I didn't know I couldn't... so I did."

"The first duty of love is to listen."

PAUL TILLICH

"IT IS THE PROVINCE OF
KNOWLEDGE TO SPEAK AND
IT IS THE PRIVILEGE OF WISDOM
TO LISTEN."

OLIVER WENDELL HOLMES

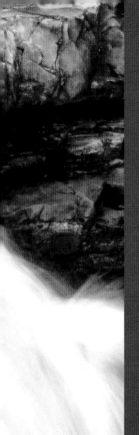

"While the right to talk may be the beginning of freedom, the necessity of listening is what makes the right important."

WALTER LIPPMANN

"IT TAKES A DISCIPLINED PERSON TO LISTEN TO CONVICTIONS WHICH ARE DIFFERENT FROM THEIR OWN."

DOROTHY FULDHEIM

CHAPTER FOUR

Play with abandon.

Watch what power play unleashes.

When I need to solve difficult business issues, I invite myself to solutions by saying, "Let's play with this a bit." Play is my most profound problem solver. Frequently I consider challenges just like a puzzle. I write out all the elements of the puzzle and literally play with them. Move them around. Create shapes with them and see how they might fit together differently than I initially imagined. Unleashing this power of play has produced remarkable results in my career as an author and trainer.

Putting a group of professionals into a play mind set…allows their capacity to be far more open to new possibilities. I admire Kevin Carroll, author of *The Red Rubber Ball*, who advocates the benefits of introducing play into the innovation process in every level of professional and personal life. My best instructor in play was my Labrador retriever, Judah. Judah agreed wholeheartedly with Carl Sandburg and Robert Frost that a gracious meandering walk was the best way to solve just about any problem.

Play also unleashes the power of teamwork. Although I played by myself as a child, my more dynamic memories of play involved the entire neighborhood…the grand sprints on our banana seat bikes, the great dramatic undertakings, kickball and treasure hunts. Those were playful enterprises that taught me a lot about team building, creating consensus and organizing group effort. To play with abandon is the first step toward extraordinary creation, remarkable solutions and breakthrough innovations. If you don't happen to have a Labrador retriever to instruct you in the best practices of play, look around for a tutor in the form of a 4-year-old. They are great teachers.

"Genius is childhood recalled at will."

CHARLES BAUDELAIRE

"Simple pleasures are the last refuge of the complex."

OSCAR WILDE

"THE 'SILLY' QUESTION IS THE FIRST INTIMATION OF SOME TOTALLY NEW DEVELOPMENT."

ALFRED NORTH WHITEHEAD

"Every child is an artist.
The problem is how to remain an artist
once he grows up."

PABLO PICASSO

"Laughter is what spills over the
edge of an inspired life."

MARY ANNE RADMACHER

"When a thing is funny,
search it for a hidden truth."

GEORGE BERNARD SHAW

"*To have the sense of creative activity
is the great happiness and the great proof
of being alive.*"

MATTHEW ARNOLD

"*The great man is he who does not
lose his child's heart.*"

MENCIUS

CHAPTER FIVE

Practice wellness.

Create your own pharmacy.

E xperts around the world offer their best assessment for you to practice wellness. But, you can create your own pharmacy—your own cabinet of "best practices" to promote your very best health and well-being.

A willingness to act from love, to spontaneously and generously express love and hold love as the highest order of good in my life created an entirely new view of my own well-being.

A big, black Labrador retriever puppy bounded into my life and began my tutorial on practicing wellness. And then a zesty, red-headed, 2-year-old joined the faculty of Practicing Wellness University. They were joined by a gift from a friend in the shape of an "ordinary" little refrigerator magnet with the words, "Never miss the opportunity to say, 'I love you.'" That team, joined by many other instructors, helped me create a personal pharmacy of wellness that I draw upon daily.

My "pharmacy" cabinet contains a variety of modalities. Let's peek in together and see if we can read some of the labels:

THE LOTION OF LOVE

SPREAD EVENLY AND OFTEN TO ACHIEVE MOST
CONSISTENT RESULTS;

INHALANT OF INSPIRATION

BREATH DEEPLY AND EXHALE SLOWLY. THIS BRINGS
CLARITY TO ALL THE PASSAGES OF YOUR LIFE;

LOZENGE OF SELF-CARE

WHEN YOU EXPERIENCE TROUBLES "SWALLOWING" OR
THERE SEEM TO BE CERTAIN ROUGH PATCHES, TAKE
THIS SOOTHING LOZENGE AND LET IT MELT AWAY
YOUR CONCERNS;

BALM OF FRIENDSHIP

THE MERE FRAGRANCE OF THIS BALSAM WILL BEGIN TO
RELIEVE SYMPTOMS. APPLY TOPICALLY FOR MORE DRA-
MATIC RESULTS;

DROPS OF MUSIC

TAKE THROUGH EARS AS OFTEN AS POSSIBLE TO
PRODUCE A LIGHTER STEP AND INVIGORATED PATTERNS
OF MOVEMENT;

EXERCISE CREAM

APPLY TO AS MANY BODY PARTS AS FREQUENTLY AS
POSSIBLE ON A CONSISTENT BASIS. FREQUENT
APPLICATION CONTRIBUTES TO AN OUTWARD VIGOR
AND AN INTERNAL VITALITY;

INJECTION OF CREATIVITY

USE WHEN PROBLEMS SEEM OVERWHELMING OR UNSOLVABLE.
INJECT DIRECTLY INTO THE IMPACTED AREA;

RESTORATIVE SLEEP CAPSULE

TAKE TWO SEVERAL HOURS BEFORE YOU PLAN TO GO
TO SLEEP. WILL ASSIST IN FORGIVING OFFENSES,
SETTING ASIDE WORRIES AND ALLOWING PROFOUND
GRATITUDE TO DESCEND BEFORE DRIFTING INTO A
DEEP, RESTORATIVE SLEEP;

EVENTUALITY CACHE

REACH INTO THE ARSENAL OF SUPPLIES AND WHAT
YOU REQUIRE FOR THE DEMAND OF THE MOMENT WILL
COME TO YOUR HAND. FOLLOW INSTRUCTIONS ON THE
LABEL AND YOUR NEED WILL, EVENTUALLY, BE MET.

Create your own pharmacy for your personal practice of wellness. What would the labels in your cabinet instruct? And on what shelf would you find love?

"LIVE STRONG."

LANCE ARMSTRONG

"Your prayer must be for a sound mind in a sound body."

JUVENAL

"*Those who don't know how to weep with their whole heart don't know how to laugh either.*"

GOLDA MEIR

"*The best doctors in the world are Doctor Diet, Doctor Quiet and Doctor Merryman.*"

JONATHAN SWIFT

"*One ought, every day at least, to hear a little song, read a good poem, see a fine picture, and, if it were possible, to speak a few reasonable words.*"

JOHANN WOLFGANG VON GOETHE

"The cure for anything is salt water: sweat, tears or the sea."

ISAK DINESEN (KAREN BLIXEN)

"*To be astonished is one of the surest ways of not growing old too quickly.*"

COLETTE (SIDONIE-GABRIELLE COLETTE)

"Don't sweat the petty things and don't pet the sweaty things."

GEORGE CARLIN

"We should not be ashamed to name what God has not been ashamed to create."

CLEMENT OF ALEXANDRIA

"If you don't do what's best for your body, you're the one who comes up on the short end."

JULIUS ERVING

6

Continue to learn.

If you learn—there is no failure.

After an extended conversation with a university president, I reflected with these words, "A key to a vital life is an eagerness to learn and a willingness to change." Rather than content yourself with what you do not know and cannot do…reach instead to celebrate what you have mastered and indeed, accomplish every day. Those things are the stepping stones to profound capacity and an unending opportunity for continued learning.

I am an artist. I am an author. I am given over easily to the humanities and complex ideas expressed through language fascinate me. Numbers? Multi-faceted computer protocols? Ah. Not so much. I used to affirm out loud, to others, "I'm computer illiterate." The assessment, while matching my experience, did not reflect my desire. I wanted to become competent on the computer. The skill set did not occur in me naturally nor come to me easily.

I began making a shift. I stopped affirming what I was not and I began saying out loud what I was willing to become. When the computer puzzled me or I made an error that lost what I was working on,

I affirmed, "I am willing to learn." "I am in the process of becoming computer literate." My words led my eagerness to learn and invited my willingness to change. I signed up for tutoring. I reinforced systems that made sense to me. I practiced. I turned my "failures" into object lessons of what not to do next time. I showed up; I took notes! In this field, I discover that the more I know...the more there is to know. The opportunity for expanding my knowledge base is always expanding. It's like climbing a mountain of information.

The saddest news to a Mazama, a passionate climber, would be that all the great heights had been conquered. But, a climber truly committed to the passion of climbing great mountains would be willing to go back and climb them all again. Why? Because there is always something new to see. The paths would have changed. The weather conditions would be variable. It would, essentially, be a fresh and challenging climb because the mountain changed and so had the climber.

"*Let us dare to read, think, speak and write.*"

JOHN ADAMS

"*Lessons are not given, they are taken.*"

CESARE PAVESE

*"Knowledge alters what we seek
as well as what we find."*

FREDA ADLER

*"I am learning all the time.
The tombstone will be my diploma."*

EARTHA KITT

"THE ONLY MEANS OF
STRENGTHENING ONE'S
INTELLECT IS TO MAKE
UP ONE'S MIND ABOUT
NOTHING–TO LET THE MIND
BE A THOROUGHFARE FOR
ALL THOUGHTS."

JOHN KEATS

7

CHAPTER SEVEN
Appreciate your friends.

...hold the hand of the world.

When I was speaking to nearly 800 very vocal and active freshmen at a High School in Arkansas, some of the faculty were actually taking bets on "how long I was going to be able to hold their attention." These freshmen were so energetic that they had not been scheduled to meet all together yet in the school year. On a particular hot, muggy April day with broken air conditioning, all of them gathered on backless bleachers for 90 minutes.

After a few minutes of telling jokes, I related a story of friendship that gave me their undivided attention for the remaining 70 of my 90 minutes. Paul David Leopoulos, the man who wrote the foreword to my book, *Lean Forward Into Your Life*, is a childhood friend of former president Bill Clinton. Paul had told me a story that deeply illustrates their friendship. This is what I told the students:

Paul David's wife called him and directed him to their local hospital. Their 17-year-old daughter, Thea, had been hit by a drunk driver. She died before he made it to the hospital.

Little Rock, while large, is a small town in the way that it behaves. Within 45 minutes of Thea's death, fellow students, neighbors and parents from the school started showing up at the house with food, hugs, and shared tears. On the hour, the phone rang. It was President Clinton. Paul David wondered how he'd found out so fast and figured he must be in town. His lifelong friend exchanged the expected sentences and then assured his pal, "I'll be there just as quick as I can."

A few hours later President Bill Clinton strode through the door. He came. He stayed. He did what his friends needed him to do. And he delivered Thea's eulogy. It was some time later that Paul David learned where President Clinton had been when he made that call—in airspace, halfway to Japan. He cancelled his calendar, turned the plane around and flew to the side of his friend.

No matter how busy... no matter how important...no matter how occupied, friends fly to their friend's side. That the friends in this story are childhood friends is the most important element. What was secondary is that one of the friends was the elected leader of the country, with enormous commitments. He understood the commitment required of him as a friend. I asked those freshmen that day, and I will ask you, "Do you turn around for your friend? And do your friends turn around for you? How do you measure your own priorities in light of the needs of your friend?"

When I stood by my father as he died, alone, with no friends...I promised myself that I would remember this, the last lesson of his life. An object lesson, really. He wished he had friends...but he had not created a structure in his later years to maintain friendships. Old cowboy wisdom says, "If you ain't got friends, you ain't got nuthin." In the affirmative, I say, "If you have one friend, you hold the hand of the world."

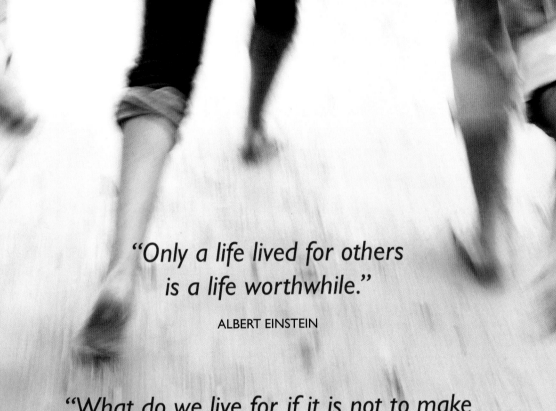

"Only a life lived for others
is a life worthwhile."

ALBERT EINSTEIN

"What do we live for, if it is not to make
life less difficult to each other?"

GEORGE ELIOT (MARY ANN EVANS)

"MANY PEOPLE WILL WALK IN

AND OUT OF YOUR LIFE...

BUT ONLY TRUE FRIENDS

WILL LEAVE FOOTPRINTS IN

YOUR HEART."

ELEANOR ROOSEVELT

8

Choose with no regret.

Own it!

It's up to you to make choices that work best for you. It really is all within your point of view. Regret is a matter of perspective. If you like who you are NOW, it follows that you can embrace, without regret, all the choices that led you here.

Difficulties impact me—they do not define me.

Challenges mold me—they do not make me.

Praise may encourage me—it is my own vision that inspires me.

Successes may spur me on but it is my own reward that satisfies me.

Pain may permeate but my heart and hope prevail.

Criticism and pettiness may knock
but the lock is on my side of the door.

Abundance may pave the road
but it is generosity that lights the way.

Lack may assail me yet it is learning the word
"enough" that assuages the hunger.

I may have a stare-down with death but I hear the
Great Voice that says, "Life begins when you do."

As long as I'm breathin' — I'm livin.'
My way. Beginning every fresh moment—now!

"Life must be lived forwards, but can only be understood backwards."

SOREN KIERKEGAARD

"Regret for the things we did can be tempered by time; it is regret for the things we did not do that is inconsolable."

SYDNEY J. HARRIS

"Choose well: Your choice is brief yet endless."

ELLA WINTER

*"Forgiveness is the act of admitting
that we are like other people."*

Christina Baldwin

*"How vain it is to sit down to write
when you have not stood up to live."*

Henry David Thoreau

*"When one door of happiness closes, another opens;
but often we look so long at the closed door that we
do not see the one which has opened for us."*

Helen Keller

9

CHAPTER NINE

Fail with enthusiasm.

Same song—new verse!

REALLY? Fail with enthusiasm? I met a young man. He was shorter than most of his peers, somewhat slight of build and yet, he seemed fearless. Not in a cowboy bravado sort of way, but as if he could face headlong anything that life blew his way.

I asked him how he came to be so brave and he said simply, "I don't mind failing. I embrace every failure as the path to success." I asked him if that didn't seem kind of defeatist to him, being so familiar with failure? He laughed and said that if I had to ask—I didn't get it.

It's taken a bit of doing but I "get it" now. Turns out it really is something I understood as a child and sort of unlearned as I "grew up." Picasso said that it takes a long time to become young. From my experience, that seems particularly true. When I was interested in climbing the tallest tree in the back yard, I quickly evaluated the various outcomes and decided it was a greater failure not to try and climb it. Many people have said that the greatest failure lies in not trying. But what about trying an action and failing WITH enthusiasm?

Being connected to my enthusiasm brings vibrancy and zest to each part of my day and throws doors wide open in my experience. There are some requirements. I must be willing to set aside my ego and any attachment I have to looking utterly competent or sophisticated. My interests must lie in discovery and presence, not appearance and assessment. The instant the familiar question, "What will people think?" is asked, enthusiasm, as well as the willingness to fail, evaporates. Enthusiasm prefers the company of freedom and unselfconsciousness.

"The greatest mistake
you can make in life is to be continually
fearing you will make one."

ELBERT HUBBARD

"THE WORLD IS BEHOLDEN TO
GENEROUS MISTAKES FOR THE
GREATEST PART OF THE GOOD
THAT IS DONE IN IT."

GEORGE SAVILE, LORD HALIFAX

"SOMETIMES THINGS GO WRONG
TO TEACH YOU WHAT IS RIGHT."

ALICE WALKER

10

Lead or follow a leader.

Remember a parade known as "you."

Will you ever know who your words and actions touch? Will you ever hear the length to which your inspiring remarks reach? Will you have the chance to see the results of the single kind gesture you extended when you thought no one was looking? Will you have a chance to feel the depth of compassion that your heart-felt generosity created? Will a grace that you blessed outward, from some deep conviction and guidance, return to you? These questions create their own answers in each heart.

When you follow a leader, you have the chance to see and enjoy the fruits of leadership—those grown on a tree of a strong and directed influence. When you are a leader, the fruit is often harvested behind you. Following and leading are essential roles in the dance of success and satisfaction. Each has its own unique reward.

When you march in a parade, you have the pleasure of seeing all those who go before you. When you lead a parade, there is no one in front of you. When you lead with confidence, perhaps some day it will be remembered that there was a parade named "You."

> *"If you want to build a ship,
> don't drum up the men to gather
> wood, divide the work and give orders.
> Instead, teach them to yearn for the
> vast and endless sea."*

ANTOINE DE SAINT-EXUPERY

> *"Ninety percent of leadership
> is the ability to communicate
> something people want."*

DIANNE FEINSTEIN

*"Keep away from people who try
to belittle your ambitions. Small people
always do that, but the really great
make you feel that you, too,
can become great."*

MARK TWAIN

*"Education is not the filling of a pail,
but the lighting of a fire."*

WILLIAM BUTLER YEATS

"A BIRD ONLY FLIES. IT DOES NOT TURN
TO ANOTHER BIRD AND ASK,
'AM I DOING THIS RIGHT?'"

MARY ANNE RADMACHER

11

CHAPTER ELEVEN

Do what you love.

...and love what you do.

Here is what this phrase means to my friend, Steve Maraboli:

Sing the song God put in your heart and don't EVER shut up!
When love is at the base of what you do, your actions create a
grand symphony that synchronizes with nature and its animated
composer. When you do what you love, the seemingly impossible
becomes simply challenging, the laborious becomes purpose-
ful resistance, the difficult loses its edge and is trampled by your
progress. When you are fueled by the endless reservoir of love, you
are connected with your truth...you have a clear vision from your
heart. Sight is the function of the eyes, but with a love-based heart
you have vision. When you do what you love, you are love.

"THE SECRET OF JOY IN WORK
IS CONTAINED IN ONE WORD:
EXCELLENCE. TO KNOW HOW
TO DO SOMETHING WELL
IS TO ENJOY IT."

PEARL S. BUCK

"If you always do what interests you,
at least one person is pleased."

KATHARINE HEPBURN

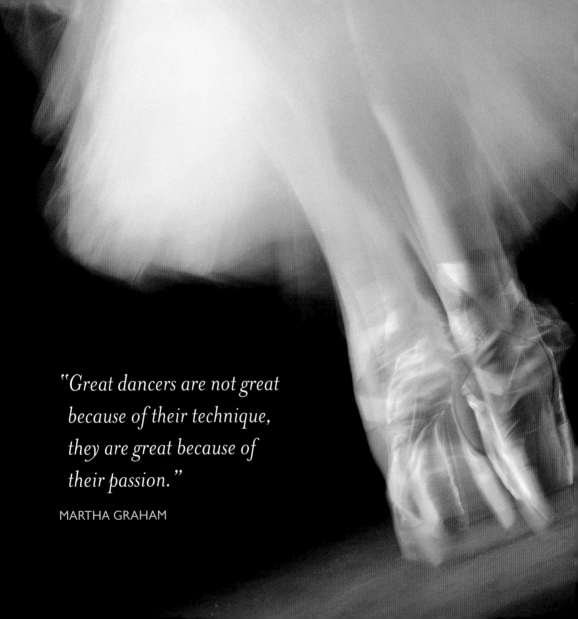

"*Great dancers are not great because of their technique, they are great because of their passion.*"

MARTHA GRAHAM

"WHEN PEOPLE GO TO WORK,
THEY SHOULDN'T HAVE TO LEAVE
THEIR HEARTS AT HOME."

BETTY BENDER

CHAPTER TWELVE

Live as if this is all there is.

Because, for NOW, it is.

> *"The universe is full of magical things, patiently waiting for our wits to grow sharper."*

EDEN PHILLPOTTS

I awakened painfully aware of the slow healing of my shoulder injury. News from one of my dearest friends put my localized pain in a larger context. Her pain was tied to cancer. Two types. Both in stage three.

On this particular day, she's thanking me for being her friend and standing by her. Thanking me for appearing in her life at the time in which she most needed my presence and my skill set. In expressing these thoughts, she was attempting to be so hopeful by presenting and embracing her "brave girl" self. I remembered an assessment of my skill set from decades earlier. I was told that I would consistently be called upon to comfort and bring courage to people who are dying. At the time I thought that was odd: We're ALL dying, right? While it may be true that we start dying the day we're born...some people have a little tighter timeline than others. It's interesting how keys from our past show up at just the moment we stand before a seemingly locked door. This is some of the magic Phillpotts is referencing.

The course of the day has kept me to the steady and schooled discipline of editing a manuscript. Not exactly the song and dance section of a hit musical. It's more like the clean up crew that goes to work after the performance is done and the theater is empty. It occurs to me that this is where the most profound magic occurs—in the ordinary...the repetitive...the predictable. To bring verve and fresh eyes to what might otherwise appear commonplace— to see the magic in the mundane.

Camus said, "You will never live if you are looking for the meaning of life." I translate to this, "To live a life of meaning–live a meaningful day. Make a meaningful choice in the immediate moment." So often we consider things in THE FUTURE and allow such a consideration to overwhelm. Considering and acting in THE NOW allows for one, immediate meaningful choice. Get a stack of those immediate meaningful choices and voila—there's meaning in your life. Simple? Yes, of course. That doesn't mean it's easy, but it is a simple truth. Meaning for the whole of your life? It begins with one meaningful choice... followed by another...and another.

And THAT begins....when YOU do.

Right now.

Go! Start!

Just like that.

Life Begins
When You Do

"How we spend our days is, of course,
how we spend our lives."

ANNIE DILLARD

"The butterfly counts not months but moments,
and has time enough."

RABINDRANATH TAGORE

"I shall not die of a cold. I shall die of having lived."

WILLA CATHER

"Don't wait for the last judgment — it takes place every day."

ALBERT CAMUS

Acknowledgments

Thanks to Mac Anderson for providing the wonderful opportunity to gather under the phrase flag of *Life Begins When You Do.* I am delighted to share a lifelong love of quotes with Mac, as well as the love of the word, "perseverance." I will always remember our conversation, with fondness, when I was explaining a complex model of intentional living involving imperatives and many "this and thats"… "Remember, the name of the company IS Simple Truths…" So simple. So true.

I appreciate Dyan, my client, allowing me to share the results of her, "Live with Intention" work with me in the form of her life-mission statement. More of Dyan's wonderful and effective work can be seen at dyaneybergen.com.

Steve Maraboli is harmony to my melody of an inspired life. He has been most generous in allowing me to share his words with you. More about his broad philanthropic and corporate work can be found at SteveMaraboli.com and Abettertoday.com.

Some whose words are included here are alive and doing amazing work in the world, such as Betty Bender and Julius Erving. Others can be explored in these ways: Kevin Carroll (kevincarrollkatalyst. com), Marion Wright Edelman (childrensdefense.org), Lance Armstrong (lancearmstrong.com), Alice Walker (alicewalkersgarden.com), Christina Baldwin (storycatcher.net), Dianne Feinstein (Feinstein.senate.gov/public/), Annie Dillard (anniedillard.com).

Learn about all the Radmacher Focus Phrase opportunities on Facebook: search for *A New Way - Radmacher Focus Phrase*.

I have gathered the quotes I share in this volume over my lifetime and have attempted to attribute them accurately. Any inaccuracies are unintentional and are my own. To those who are living and celebrated on these pages, thank you for the wisdom that you have provided in my life.

 Mary Anne Radmacher has been contributing inspiring, memorable words to the publishing and gift industry for almost thirty years. In addition to her friendship with SimpleTruths.com, she largely publishes with Red Wheel•Weiser•Conari Press. She has formed many artful licensing relationships...among them Quotable Cards, Brushdance, Demdaco, maryanneradmacher.com, Juststickemup.com, Hot Off The Press and My Spirit Garden.

From the time she conducted her first "performance piece" by filling the wall in her family breakfast nook when she was two - she has been compelled to bring sense and meaning to her view of the world with words and graphic form. She considers herself first a writer, then a trainer and finally, an artist. She insists her friendship with art exists because she sees all form as symbol, including color and the alphabet. She forms a cohesive whole when she partners all the symbolic elements available to her vivid imagination. She says, "I create from that place where silence and meaning meet." Throughout her career she has maintained consistent messaging - that each person, alone, is responsible for the way in which they travel the world. And as an underscore to that - she believes that one person can not only make a difference but that the world's health depends on single individuals committing to making a profound impact on their immediate world.

In LIFE BEGINS WHEN YOU DO Mary Anne reflects on one of her best loved pieces, LIVE WITH INTENTION, offering up a nurturing bowl of inspiring, thoughtful soup for the spirit. When Mac Anderson mentioned the title for the piece he wanted her to create, she immediately went to work. Over the first few months she created a work of large proportion. Research. Cross referencing. Intense narrative. Exercises. Whew! Mac and Mary Anne discussed a sample chapter she had sent along. Kindly, but with the tender forthrightness on which he has built his career, Mac suggested that the content was far more complex than he had initially imagined.

With a soft nudge, Mac reminded Mary Anne, "After all, the company IS called Simple Truths."

Then the real work began! Mary Anne distilled, condensed and offered the most illustrative core of each of her compelling Intentional tenets. What you hold here is an inspiring direct invitation to live close to your intention, to call yourself to begin the true work of your life NOW - not waiting for "other" circumstances or a more appropriate time. This book declares that the life you've always longed for is waiting for you somewhere...it's ready to begin when you are!

The
simple truths®
DIFFERENCE

If you have enjoyed this book we invite you to check out our entire collection of gift books, with free inspirational movies, at **www.simpletruths.com.** You'll discover it's a great way to inspire friends and family, or to thank your best customers and employees.

For more information, please visit us at:

www.simpletruths.com

Or call us toll free... 800-900-3427